CHIKASHA

VOLUME THREE: SHARED WISDOM

S·T·O·R·I·E·S

CHIKASHA

— VOLUME THREE: SHARED WISDOM —

S·T·O·R·I·E·S

BY GLENDA GALVAN · ILLUSTRATIONS BY JEANNIE BARBOUR

Chickasaw Press

CHIKASHA STORIES, VOLUME THREE: SHARED WISDOM

© Copyright 2013 by Chickasaw Press

ISBN 978-1-935684-09-1

Book Design: Skip McKinstry
Cover Design: Skip McKinstry, Aaron Long

Chickasaw Press
PO Box 1548
Ada, Oklahoma 74821
www.chickasawpress.com

DEDICATIONS

*Once upon a time there was a woman who had
the most important things her heart desired.
That would be me. This book is dedicated to
my two precious sons, Steven and Nicholas,
and to my humble, Spirit-filled husband, Tino.
Their encouragement and total support
throughout the process of getting the stories
ready for this publication was amazing!*

GLENDA GALVAN

*I dedicate this book to my Mom, who has always
pointed me in the direction of my dreams.*

JEANNIE BARBOUR

CONTENTS

GLENDA GALVAN:
ABOUT STORYTELLING

Chickasaws, and many other tribal people, talk of a kindred spirit with the animals of the earth and looked to them for wisdom. I've always felt a kinship with wildlife, and our tribal stories locked in the connection between our totems and the relationships our ancestors had with the animal kingdom. In our world, traditionally, we watched the animals keenly as our lives depended on the knowledge gained from these survivors.

Most animals are endowed with certain characteristics. Chickasaws tried to imitate these behaviors, especially those most admired by our medicine people and our leaders. Traditional Chickasaws didn't learn about the animal. Rather, we learned from the animal.

Elders sometimes share stories and oral histories involving experiences with animals and life learning situations. Often, these stories explain why things are the way they are such as how raccoon got his ringed tail, and how wasp got the poison he carries even today. Our clan system is set predominantly around the animal kingdom with the deer clan, fox clan, beaver clan, and bird clan. The better I got to know these stories, the closer I felt to our ancestors.

It was quite difficult to put the stories in writing because I depend on the audience to know which stories I might share with them. Seeing the excitement of those in front of me as we share this cultural experience is an experience that never gets old.

Our journey through this life knows no finite borders, nor does it have a clear path to follow. Stories contained in these pages are part of our ancient culture, a place where I have always felt safe and can still find myself among our ancestors. These stories can strengthen the bonds that connect generations as they have for me.

ACKNOWLEDGEMENTS

Many people have helped me make this book a reality, and while I wish I could list them each and every one, I will acknowledge as many as possible. I am very grateful for the time given to me by a great number of tribal elders who love to share oral histories with those who take the time to listen to them. I am most humbled to call so many of them "friends."

I always had encouragement and support from my family. Their unconditional love truly is representative of a Chickasaw family for it's the perpetuation of families that keeps our tribe alive and well. Special love and appreciation go to my husband, Tino; sons, Steven and Nick; and daughter-in-law, McKae. I cannot describe the unwavering love from my mother and sisters. Mom, you believed in me and this project and I thank you for always being there. Lorie Robins has carried many of our stories to all parts of our Nation, and she has become the daughter I never had.

I'd like to dedicate this last book to the memory of my dad, Tom Taylor, and to my two grandchildren, Anna and Thiago.

Finally, heartfelt appreciation to Josh Hinson and the dedicated Chickasaw language speakers, Chickasaw Press, and my long-time friend and awesome artist, Jeannie Barbour. May you be truly blessed!

GLENDA GALVAN

JEANNIE BARBOUR: ABOUT ILLUSTRATING STORIES

I have thoroughly enjoyed working on the illustrations for the *Chikasha Stories* volumes of books. The work has pushed me in new directions of growth not only as an artist, but also as a tribal citizen wishing to gain further understanding of our wonderful culture and history. Each story is simple in its purity of message. Through the illustration process, I have tried to infuse each character with that same sense of purity. As always, I am awed by the great wisdom of our ancestors and thankful they chose to share these stories so that we may know better what it means to be Chickasaw.

ACKNOWLEDGEMENTS

I thank God for making me Chickasaw and for allowing me to serve Chickasaw people in the work I have had the privilege of doing for the past twenty-six years. I am grateful to Governor Bill Anoatubby for his vision, leadership, and support of Southeastern art in its many forms. His commitment to the creation of arts-based classes, programs, and events, is the launch pad from which the next generation of Native artists will spring. I'm also thankful for my good friend Glenda Galvan. She has committed her life to the preservation and revitalization of Chickasaw history, culture, and language. Generations of Chickasaws will benefit from the work she has done. I am thankful for having such a great son, mom, friends, and family—all of whom have supported me through thick and thin. Lastly, I am eternally grateful to the Chickasaw Press. Their devotion to excellence is second to none. They have helped make this three-year project a true adventure and great blessing in my life.

JEANNIE BARBOUR

NOTE ON CHICKASAW LANGUAGE
INTERPRETATION IS A TRICKY BUSINESS

We use the word *interpretation,* rather than *translation,* quite purposefully. When these stories were retold in English, things changed somewhat, and they change again when we go back to the original Chickasaw language. Interpreters have to be careful about keeping the important parts intact and bringing back some of the richness that gets lost in translation.

These are not literal, word-for-word translations from English to Chickasaw. Such translations would be unintelligible to a native speaker of Chickasaw. Instead, what we have strived to do is put Chickasaw stories, retold in English, back into a Chickasaw form that reflects the conventions of Chickasaw oral tradition. We've tried to give them a voice that sounds like how the old folks, *kamassa,* would've said them. We hope you will enjoy them.

Chokma'shki, yakkookay,

JOANN ELLIS AND JERRY IMOTICHEY,
WITH JOSHUA D. HINSON AND DR. JOHN DYSON

CHIKASHA

VOLUME THREE: SHARED WISDOM

STORIES

CROW
AND
HAWK

AS TOLD TO RUTH BENEDICT

This story is dedicated
to all parents and grandparents,
whether natural, adoptive, or
foster. My husband and I
are foster parents and this
piece serves as a reminder
of how important families
and bonding should be
to each of us.

CROW HAD A NEST

and had been sitting on her eggs for many days.

But she got tired of sitting there, and she flew away.

While she was gone,

Hawk came by day

after day after day

and found

no one sitting on the nest of eggs. Hawk said to herself, "The person who owns this nest no longer cares for it. I am sorry for those eggs lying in that empty nest. I will sit on those poor little eggs and they will be my children."

She sat many days on the eggs and no one came to the nest to check on them. Finally, they began to hatch. Still, no Crow came. The little ones all hatched out, and the mother Hawk flew about getting food for them. They grew bigger and bigger, and their wings got strong. At last, the mother Hawk took the little ones off the nest.

At this time, Crow remembered her nest and came back to it. She found all her eggs had hatched, and Hawk was taking care of her little ones. One day she met Hawk out feeding with her little ones. "Hawk!" "Yes, what is it you want?" "You must return these little ones you're leading around." "Why did you leave them?" asked Hawk. "Because they are mine," said Crow. "Yes, you laid the eggs, to be sure, but you had no pity on them when you left and never returned to see that they had proper care," replied Hawk. "You went off and left them, and I came and sat upon the nest and hatched them. When they were hatched, I fed them and now I lead them about. They are mine, and I shall not return them." Crow and Hawk argued back and forth until Hawk finally said to Crow, "I shall not give them up. I have worked for them, and for many days I have fasted sitting there upon the eggs. In all that time you did not come near your eggs. Why is it now that I have taken care of the little ones and brought them up and they have grown that you want them back?" "Come, my children, for I am your mother," said Crow, but the little ones answered, "We do not know you. Hawk is our mother."

When Crow could not make the little ones understand, she told Hawk they would go to court to get their answer. Hawk answered, "That is good. I am willing, and we shall see who has the right to these little ones."

So mother Crow took mother Hawk before Eagle, chief of the bird clan. Eagle said to Crow, "Why did you leave your nest?" The Crow hung her head and had nothing to say. At last Crow said, "When I came back to my nest, I found my eggs already hatched and the Hawk taking charge of the little ones. I have come to ask that the Hawk be required to return the children to me." Eagle asked of Hawk, "How many times did you find this nest

of eggs?" "Many times I came to this nest of eggs and found it empty. No one came for a long time, and at last I took pity on the poor little eggs. I said to myself, 'The mother who made this nest can no longer care for these eggs. I should be glad to hatch these little ones.' I worked hard and brought them up and they have grown." Mother Crow interrupted mother Hawk and said, "But these are my children. I laid the eggs." Mother Hawk answered, "We are both asking for justice and it will be given to us." "Is that all?" asked Eagle. "Yes, I have worked hard to raise my little ones. Just when they were grown, mother Crow came back and asked to have them back again, but I shall not give them back. It is I who fasted and worked, and now they are my little ones."

The chief of the bird clan said, "The mother Hawk is not willing to return the little ones to the mother Crow, and if you really had pity on your little ones, why did you leave your nest for so many days and are now demanding them back? The mother Hawk is the mother of the little ones for she has fasted and hatched them and flew about searching out their food, and now they are her children."

Mother Crow said to Eagle, chief of the bird clan, "You should ask the little ones which mother they will follow." So Eagle asked the little ones which mother they chose. The little ones answered together, "Mother Hawk is our mother! She is all the mother we know." The little Crow children said, "In the nest you had no pity on us, and you left us. Mother Hawk hatched us, and she is our mother."

So it was finally settled as the little ones had finally chosen that they were the children of Mother Hawk, who had pity on them in the nest and brought them up. Mother Crow began to weep. "Do not weep," said Eagle, chief of the bird clan. "It is your own fault that you have lost your children, because you left the nest. It is the final decision of the bird clan that these little ones shall go with the Mother Hawk." And so it was.

FALA' MICHA AKANKABI'

AS TOLD TO RUTH BENEDICT

Ishtanompa' yappat inki'; ishki',
imafo'si', ippo'si', chipota finha'
ki'yokmat chipota habina' micha
chipota apiisachi' holiitoblichi.
Ahattak micha anaat chipota
ilapiisachi, micha ishtanompa
yappat haponokfónkachi
kanihmit chokka – chaffa'
micha ittibaachaffaka ayyoko'li
ponchokma'hi bíyyi'ka.

FALA'AT PICHIK

intálla'attook<u>o</u> nittak kanohmi alaata. Bínni'likat

tikahbi tahacha wakaat kaniyattook. Aba' kaniyak<u>a</u>

Akankabi'at nittak kanohmi

wakaa ootayahmat

akankoshi'<u>a</u> kanookya

ikombinni'lo

29

himmaka písttook. Kanoat pichikat immi'hookmat

apiisachi ki'yo. Ankankoshi' sawa alhiha'

ihokhánglo Akankabi'at aashttook. Akankoshi'

iskanno'si ilbashsha ombiniilila'chi micha

anchipota'chi.

Akankabi'at nittak kanohmi ala tattook micha

kanookya pichik iko'no. Akankoshi' apiisachikat.

Himmakahma hofanti hooishtayattook, yahmikya

Fala'at iklo. Móma hofanti taha Akankabishkaat

wakaat impa' hoyo ishtimala. Hoohichitohmacha

ifanalhchi'at kilimpi taha. Himmakahma

Akankabishkaat s̲awa alhiha aatilhilittook.

Falakaashoot yahmihm̲a impichik nokfokhacha
Falahmat onattook. Imakankoshi' m̲ómat hofanti
taha micha Akankabi'at inchipota apiisachit
ahánta hayooshttook. Nittak chaffa' Akankabi'
micha chipota hooittibaaimpat tánno'wana. Falaat
afamattook "Akankabi'!" "Ii, nanta chibanna?"
"S̲awa'si' ishpilichik̲a ishfalamacha'shki." "Katihmit
ish̲ifalamitok?" Akankabi'at imasilhhattook.
"Ammi'hootok̲o," Falaat aashttook. "Ii, akankoshi'
ishchiilittook nanna ishtikchinkanihmokat
chikapiisachokittook ishima kaniyattook,"
Akankabi'at imaachi. "Ishaakaniyak̲a anakoot
alaatalittook hofantachili. Hofantik̲a, ipitalit
pilishlittook. Ammi' chifalamichila'chi ki'yo."

Fala' micha Akankabi'at hooittichapana
Akankabi'at Fala imaachihmat "Ch̲ifalamachila'chi
ki'yo. Intoksalili micha nittak lawa' Akankabi'

ombiniililit okissalittook. Yahmika akankoshi' milinka' chikonokittook. Katihmi himmakahma hofantichilicha hichito tahaka falamachit chibanna?"

"Chipota, hoominti', anakoot hoochishki' saya" Falaat imaachi, chipotaat aachihmat "Akchitha'no. Akankabi'akoot poshki!"

Falaat sawa'si' alhiha' kostinichi ki'yohmat, Akankabi' imaachihma "Nanna alhpisa'akoot imanompa falamicha'chihookya." "Yamma chokma micha ayyopánshli, kanimpit chipota ishaachika ilipisa'chi."

Fala'at Akankishki' Osi' tikba ishtonattook. Osaat Fala imaachihmat: "Katihmat chimpichik ishaakaniyataam?" Falaat ishkobo takaachit nanna ikaacho'kittook. Himmakahma Falaat aachihmat: "Falamat alalika Akankabi'at akankoshi' hofantichi tahacha sawa' alhiha apiisachit ahántatok. Akankabi'at chipota afalamacha'chi anhili." Osaat Akankabi' imasilhhahmat "Katohmi akankoshi' ishhayoshtaam? Nittak kanohmi pichik onalik<u>a</u> akankoshi' alhihaat alhtotok kanookya iklokitok. Haatok<u>o</u> akankoshi' <u>i</u>nokhángolitok. Ilaashlihmat "Ishkaat fichik ikbitokat makahm<u>a</u> nanna ishtinkanihmot ikhofanticho. Hofantichila'chikat asayoppa'hi bíyya'ka. Kallo toksalili hofantichilik<u>a</u> hichito taha." Falashkaat Akankabishki' ataklammit aachihmat "Anchipota anakoot akankoshi' chiilitok." Akankabi'at aachihm<u>a</u>, "Iitáwwa'at nannahoot alhpí'sa pobannatok<u>o</u> ilisha'chi." "Yammak illataa?" <u>O</u>saat asilhha. "<u>I</u>i, kallo toksalilit s<u>a</u>wa' alhiha hofantichilitok hofanti taha finhak<u>a</u> Falaishkaat falamat alacha chipota alhiha banna, <u>i</u>falamachila'chi ki'yo. Himmak<u>o</u>'n<u>o</u> s<u>a</u>wa'si' ammi' toksalili micha okissalitok<u>o</u>." Foshi Iksa' <u>I</u>minkaat aachihmat, "Akankabishkaat falamat s<u>a</u>wa' alhiha Falaishki' ima ikbanno, s<u>a</u>wa' ish<u>i</u>nokhánglotokmat katihmit nittak kannohmi' ishaakaniyatok micha ch<u>i</u>falamat

chibanna?" Akankabi'akoot s̲awa'si' ishki'
yammakoot ikimpot toksalicha hofantichitok micha
impa i̲hoyotok Akankabi' hootok̲o inchipota."

Falashkaat Minko O̲si' imaachihmat
"S̲awa'si alhiha imasilhhashki' katimpi' pilicha'ni
banna" O̲saat imasilhhahm̲a táwwa'alinchit
"Akankabi'akoot poshki'! Ishki' yammak illa ilithá̲na.
Pichiik ilaa-aashak̲a ishhi' ponokhánglokitok
ishponkaniyatok. Akankabishkaat apolaatalitokoot
poshki'."

Haatok̲o himmakahm̲a hooittibaachaffatok
Falaat yaa ishtayahm̲a, O̲si' I̲minko' aachihmat
"Ishyaanna. Pichik ishaakaniyatok̲o chipota
hachikaniya." Foshi Iksa'at anompa alhpí'sa
isht̲álhlhi, s̲awa' alhiha Akankabishki'ak̲o
ibaa-aya'chi, aachi," miya.

SPARKS OF LIFE

This account has been
re-told for many years
although we cannot
locate the source. It
serves as a reminder
of the compassion
Aba' Binni'li'
impressed on
our elders.

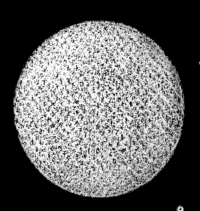

IN A CHICKASAW TOWN

lived an old, old man who had served his people

in his younger days in wars and helped his people

in many ways, but now was growing feeble and could not go about anymore. But his opinion was sought on many things, for he was a wise man for his time. Some asked him if he could tell them anything about the spirits and this old man said: "Yes, I can tell all of you people. Come and sit here on the grass while I tell you about them."

"We are all sparks from Aba' Bínni'li'. He scatters us out here and there to make lights in the towns and when it pleases Him, He gathers us up again. When we die, our spark goes to Him, and if it pleases him we are sent back. The good spirits and the evil spirits both come back here again, but only the good ones can help others, for the bad ones are just dead sparks and can do nothing. The

time when the bad ones could do anything was

before they left here the first time. After they go

away once, they can only come back and let you

hear them, but they can do you no harm, for their

power is gone. They are just like the sparks from

the fire; they shine a little while and then they do

not shine. Aba' Bínni'li' is the only power here.

What He does is good, and the spirits He sends to

us are the good ones. You know the spirits come,

because you both see and hear them at night. You

think that because you hear them at night, they

are evil spirits, but that is only because it is night.

The spirits who come from Aba' Bínni'li' come

to do you good and bring you a message from another spirit to your spirit to let you know what it is you should do."

"I am an old man and I have seen some good warriors and some fierce warriors go to the death, and I have met their spirits after that. The message they brought, when I could understand it, was a good message. I have believed the message, and have tried to do what was brought to me. Now you who have friends and family who have gone on, see if you do not find a good spirit who will bring us only what we need to keep us alive, for the good spirit will bring us only what we need. The good spirits are everywhere. They come and gather up the other sparks for Aba' Bínni'li' and take them back to where they started, so as to

make one big blaze in the fireplace where all join

and send out one big light to show us where the

house of Aba' Bínni'li' is. These spirits come back

here to gather up the wandering sparks to keep

them all together for us so we will know where

they are. We must not be afraid of them, for they

know we are akin to them.

I go myself soon to make big, bright light

with Aba' Bínni'li'.

OKCHÁA SHOKMALALLI'

An<u>o</u>li' yappa
yahmi kanohmi
an<u>o</u>wattookookya
kanoht tingba
an<u>o</u>littook<u>a</u> ilihayoocho.
Anompa' yappat
pomanokfihí̱licha'chi
Aba' Bínni'li'at
p<u>o</u>sipokni' alhiha
áyya'shak<u>a</u>
<u>i</u>nokhánglok<u>a</u>.

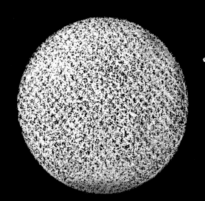

Hattak Sipoknaat

Chikashsha aachompa' ahántahminattook

lókko'li áyya'shaka himitta katihmikat tannap

ittibicha nanna ila ishtapilahminattook.

Himmako'no ikilimpo ishtayatoko kaniyookya

aya ki'yo. Hookya nanna lawa' anokfíllika,

imahaklo bannahminattook hattak

hopoyoksattooko. Kanihkat shilombish

alhiha aayimmika imasilhha anhihmat

hooimasilhhattook. Hattak sipoknaat, "Ii,

hashmóma hachimanoli bíyyi'ka," aachi.

"Minticha hashshok ombiniili nanna móma

ayahma hachimanolilika."

Iliimómat shokmalalli' hapoya Aba'

Bínni'li'ako aaminti. Poittafi'mopa yahmikma

aachompa' aayókko'lika shoppala' hapoayatok

micha Aba' Bínni'li'at ishtayoppalínchikma

shokmallali'at Aba' Bínni'li' imifilammi micha

ishtayoppánchikmat falamat anowa yappa iiminti.

Shilombish chokma' micha chioppolo' tamowa

yappa hooalahookya Shilombish Chokma' alhihaat

nanna chokma bíyyi'ka, shilombish oppolo'

alhihahookano shokmalalli' illi'ootoko nanna

kanihma ki'yo. Kaniya fokha nanna hooyahmi

bíyyi'kakat tíngba hooaakaniyokat í'maka

ámmo'na kaniyokmat falamat alakma ishhaklo illa

hoochihottopachi ki'yo. Ishkilimpi hooinkaniya.

Chipashi' hoochimmi kanihmo'si shokmalalla'cha

makkahma shokmalalli ki'yo. Yapppa Aba'

Bínni'li'akillaat kilimpi nanna kanihmikma

chokma micha shilombish hapopilichika mómaat

chokma. Shilombish alhihaat kanihmat alataha

oklhilikma hashpisa'chi micha hashhakla'chika.

Hashithána micha anokfillikmat oklhiliako

hashhánglootoko shilombish oppolo chimahooba.

Alhihat Shilombish, Aba' Bínni'li' aamintikat

chinchokma'chicha hachimala micha Shilombish

ila'at chishilombish nanna ishkanihma'chika

anompa hachima.

Hattak sipokni' saya, haatakoot tashka

chokma' micha tashka issikopa' támmowa

ayat illi písli micha ishilombish afammalitok.

Anompa akostinichilikma anompa chokmatok.

Yamma yimmilitoko nanna aachika yahmi

mihali. Yahmitoko himmaka' hachishno, inkána

micha ishchionchiloli' hooloshomattooka;

shilombish chokma' hashhayoocha'nika nanna

hapobannaakilla hapomala'chi yahmikma

hapokchaacha'chi. Kaniookya shilombish

chokmakat áyya'sha micha alacha shokmalalli

alhiha ittafamo'licha Aba' Bínni'li' intifamolicha

falamat kaniyo aamintitoka falamat ishtaya tahli

yahmikma lowak ishto' chaffa' hooittibaachaffacha

shoppala ishto' chaffa' shokkawalichi kaniya Aba'

Bínni'li' inchokkaat tálla'haka hapopisacha'chi

shilombish alhihakat falamat alacha shilombish

yoshobaka ittafammo'li tahakma kaniyaho

áyya'shaka ilithána'chika ilinokshopa'chi ki'yo,

iliikánnohmikat hooithána'chi.

Anaakya chikosikma ayali shoppala ishto'

Aba' Bínni'li' ibaaikbila'chi.

HOW TURKEY GOT HUMAN HAIR

W E KNOW RABBIT

and Terrapin had their race and how Terrapin won that race. Well, Terrapin was still celebrating his victory and decided to go hunting. He took a couple of his brothers with him, and they soon headed back to their town with plenty to eat. Just before they got

to the river, they spied something lying on the pathway in front of them. It was locks of hair, and the terrapins felt sure it was from the Chickasaws who lived down the river. Terrapin picked them up and carried them over his shoulder, thinking he would tell the whole town about how brave he had been when they encountered the Chickasaws.

Along came Turkey, who spied the dried meat over their shoulders. He tried to talk them out of some of it, saying he had been out hunting and had no luck because the terrapins had hunted and left nothing for him.

Terrapin and his brothers didn't want to share, but since they had plenty, they decided to give Turkey a little of their dried meat. Turkey noticed the locks of hair and inquired about how they had taken it from the Chickasaws. The terrapins told Turkey they had battled the Chickasaw hunters for the meat and had won, just like they had won the race against Rabbit earlier. Now Turkey just knew if he had those locks of hair, he could have any pretty girl he wanted, and he was looking for a wife.

He asked Terrapin if he could at least look at the hair. Terrapin told him no, and they began to move down the path, again bragging to one another.

Turkey told Terrapin at least to let him show the brothers that the hair would look better if they wore it draped around their necks. They finally gave some of the hair to Turkey, who proceeded to place the locks around his neck, all the while inching backward, very slowly, until he was away from the three terrapins. He finally took off running with the locks around his neck. The terrapins were quick and precise with their tiny bows and arrows, shooting Turkey in both legs, crippling him.

To this day, Turkey has the locks of Chickasaw hair around his neck and splinters in his legs. That is why a chicken leg contains one big bone unlike his brother, the turkey.

CHALOKLOWAAT
HATTAK
IPASHI'
ÍSHTTOOK

CHOKFI' LOKSI' TÁWWA'AT

Cittimpalammicha Loksi'at imambittook miya. Haatoko Loksi'at imambikat chokmakat í'macha owwatta ayattook. Inakfish ibaa-ayacha nipi' ilawa' hayoochit aachompa' falamattook. Abookoshi' ikonnokishahmat hinoshi' nanna tí'wa písttook miya. Ipashí'attook.

Chikashsha aashakat abookoshi' milinka'si'k<u>a</u> ipashi' imahoobattook. Ishcha shaalihmat aikl<u>o</u>ha imanoola'ni, Chikashsha ittafamahmat.

Haatok<u>o</u> Chaloklowaat mihíntihmat shakba' nipi' shila' ontí'wak<u>a</u> pisattook. Ishi miyattookat aachikat owwattahookya nannikayyocho loksi' alhihaat owwattahootok<u>o</u>.

Loksi' ịnakfish cho'maat nipi' shila'

ịlawattook miya. Ittinkashabla'ni ikbannohookya

kanihmo'si imattook. Chaloklowaat ipạshi'

pischa katịshtchi Chikashsha ipạshi' íshttook

imasilhhattook. Loksi' cho'maat imaachikat

Chikashsha owwatta' nipi' shila' ishtittibicha

imambittook, Chokfi' ittimpalammicha chohmi

aashtook. Chaloklowaat ipạshi' ịshikmat ihoo

chokma'sihookya bannakmat isha'hi bíyyi'ka

ithánakạ. Ihoo hoyottook miya.

Chaloklowaat Loksi' imasilhhakat ipạshi'

pisa'ni imasilhhattookạ ki'yo aashttook.

Loksi' cho'maat aiklọhaat áa ishtayahookya

Chaloklowaat imaachihmat ipạshi' pisa chokma'ni

ímmayya, nokhistap apokfohlikm<u>a</u> aashttook.

Chaloklow<u>a</u> kaniht í'mana ip<u>a</u>shi' nokhistap

apokfoh<u>ó</u>lit bakhitiblittook miya. Loksi' hopaaki

onnahmat kaniht malit ishtaya ip<u>a</u>shi' nokhistap

apokfohli tahlittook miya. Loksi' cho'maat

t<u>o</u>shpa'si tanamp<u>a</u>lhlhi naki' táww<u>a</u>'a iyyi' nalhlhi,

imomopollo tahattook miya.

Yammak<u>o</u> himmaka' Chaloklowaat

Chikashsha ip<u>a</u>shi' nokhistap apakfota micha

iyyi'at foni' oshkochcha chohmi. Akankaat iyyi'

foni' ishto' chaffa'si, <u>i</u>nakfish Chaloklowa chohmi

ki'yo miya. Yammak illa.

HOW TROUBLE CAME

TO THE CHICKASAWS

Mr. Alligator was

sunning himself on a log when Rabbit came up to him and said, "Mr. Alligator, have you ever seen the trouble?" "No, Mr. Rabbit, I have not seen the trouble, but I'm not afraid of trouble and you can tell him so." Rabbit the trickster was jealous of Alligator. Why should

he be able to live both on land and in the water?

Besides, he always seemed so happy and content

with whatever he was doing.

So, Rabbit told Alligator to follow him high

up on a hill, hoping to take Alligator so far away

from the water that he wouldn't make it back alive.

But lo and behold, Alligator traveled back to the

water without any problem. "I just thought if you came up the hill you'd see trouble," said Rabbit. Disappointed, Rabbit had to come up with another plan to get Alligator back up the hillside.

A few days later, Rabbit came by to visit Alligator. "Now Mr. Alligator, if you see something rising towards the sky, don't be afraid, for trouble will just be starting out," said Rabbit. "Now don't you worry about me, because I don't get scared. And when you see the deer running and the birds flying past you, don't get scared," Rabbit told Alligator.

The next day Rabbit started a fire nearby on top of the hill and called to Alligator for help. Alligator quickly got out of the warm water and headed for Rabbit, who was hidden in tall grass on the side of the next hill. Alligator smelled smoke but did not recognize the smell, since he'd never known fire or smoke. As he crawled toward Rabbit's voice, the heat from the fire burned his beautiful skin. Alligator used to have the most beautiful skin, creamy white and smooth. He was also a happy fellow, spending his days swimming in the river or roaming the land. When he finally got back to the water, his skin was cracked, wrinkled, and a muddy dark brown. Rabbit was laughing hard and slapping his knees, because Alligator was so ugly. By then, Alligator realized he'd been tricked.

This is how trouble came to us. Never before did we have trouble with fire. It was sacred, and we only used it for cooking and warmth. However, thanks to Rabbit the trickster, this is how we first got trouble.

KANIHT ATAKLAMA'AT

CHIKASHSHA IMALATTOOK

Hachọ'chaba'at toominni

Hitti' tapa' ontí'wana Chokfaat ala micha imaachihmat:

"Hachọ'chaba' himonnahookya ataklama' ishpísa?"

"Ki'yo, Chokfi', Ataklama' akpi'sohookya

iṉokshoopali ki'yo micha ishimanọli bíyyi'ka.

Haksichi' Chokfaat Hachọ'chaba'a ishtịhopoo

imịlitokọ. Katihmiht Hachọ'chaba'at yaakni'

micha oka' táwwa'a atta? Yahmihmat ayoppa

micha nanna alhpí'sa bíyyi'ka nannookya

kanihmikm<u>a</u>.

Haatak<u>o</u> Chokfaat Hach<u>o</u>'chaba' iman<u>o</u>likmat

issáwwali'china onchaba' aachaaha' iliontiya'chi

nanna ahnikat Hach<u>o</u>'chaba'at oka' <u>i</u>hopaaki

salamikat falamat okch<u>a</u>'at onnachi ki'yo.

Haatookya Hacho̲'chaba'at nanna ikinkanihmot falamat oka' onattook. "Nanna anokfihíllikat sakti' ishtoyyakmat ataklama'a̲ ishpisa'ni, amahoobatok," Chokfaat aachi. Ikhimonnatoko̲, Chokfaat nanna i̲la kanisht Hacho̲'chaba'a̲ falamahat sakti' aatoyya'chika̲.

Kanihmo'si' abanapaka Chokfikaashoot Hacho̲'chaba' inchokkaalattook. "Taa, Hacho̲'chaba, nannahmat shotik pilla abawa ishpísakma̲ chimilhlhanna ataklamahookoot himonna kochchat minti," Chokfaat aachi. 'Taa, anookano̲ ishtissanokfihíli̲na sa̲nokshoopa ki'yo micha issi' tilhaa micha foshi' hoowakaa ishpísaka̲ chimilhlhanna," Chokfaat Hacho̲'chaba' imaachittook.

Onnaka̲ Chokfaat onchaba' milinka' pakna'a̲ lowak ooticha Hacho̲'chaba' i̲waa apilachika̲. Hacho̲'chaba'at to̲shpat oka' lashpa' aakochchacha Chokfi' apila aya. Chokfaat sakti ootapoota hashshok chaaha' anonka' lohmacha wáyyattook. Hacho̲'chaba'at shobooli oshshowanchihookya nannaka̲ ikitha'no himonnookya lowak micha shobooli ikpi'sotoko̲.

Chokfi' įnonka yamma pilla balallit aya lowakat įhakshop chokma'si' hoshbalit ishtaya. Hacho̱'chaba' įhakshopat chokma'si' ímmayya įshihminattook, tohómbi micha lhimishkottook. Oka' yopi' micha yaakni' folo'kachicha imittakanchikat ayoppatok. Himmakana oka' onnaka̱ įhakshopat kishafa, koyoha micha lokchok bíyyi'kacha, lakna losayyi. Chokfaat kanihka̱ ollalicha iyyintolhka'pasáa Hacho̱'chaba'at pisayoba ki'yotoko̱. Himmakana Hacho̱'chabakaashoot ootkostini haksichitoko̱.

Haatoko̱ yakohmit ataklahmat pomalattook. Himonnookya lowakat ikpontaklamokitok. Holittopa' micha ishilihopooni micha polashpachiakillattook. Hookya, Haksichi' Chokfi'ako̱ yakkookay ilimaachi, yakohmachi tingba ataklama ilooshittook.

ABA' BÍNNI'LI'

In July of 1736, John Wesley
gave a very good written
account of an interview with
five Chickasaw warriors
who were on their way back
from Savannah, Georgia
by canoe. This story comes
from that account.

A VERY LONG TIME AGO,

Chickasaws learned to organize their lives according to motions of the sun, the moon, and the stars. This is how they learned to schedule their ceremonies, planting, harvest, hunting, and fishing. But it was Aba' Bínni'li', or "He that lives in the clear sky," who provided inspiration for daily life on earth.

Mr. Wesley asked, "Do you believe there is one above who is over all things?" One of the warriors answered, "We believe there are four beloved things above; the clouds, the sun, the clear sky, and 'He that lives in the clear sky.'"

When asked if Aba' Bínni'li' also made the sun and other beloved things, the warriors agreed they could not say for sure as no one had seen Aba' Bínni'li'. They did agree, however, that he had made people from the "ground."

Mr. Wesley asked the warriors if Aba' Bínni'li' had not often saved their lives from their enemies. Each of the warriors gave examples of times in war and battles when bullets and arrows had gone on this side and that side but none had hurt any of them. "And if I am to die, I shall die, and I will die like a man. But if he will have me to live, I shall live. Tho' I have never seen so many enemies, He can destroy them all," said one of the warriors.

When asked how these warriors came to have the knowledge they had regarding such revelations, they answered this way: "Ever since we came to the place we call home, the knowledge has been with us. We are young men; the old men know more. But all of them do not know. There are but a few whom Aba' Bínni'li' chooses from a child, and the knowledge is in them and he takes care of them and teaches them. They know these things and our old men practice them; therefore we know little."

ABA' BÍNNI'LI'

Hopaakikaashookano
hashi' Cholaay holhchifoat,
afammi 1736, John Wesleyat
tashka' Chikashsha
talhlhá'pi' ittafamana nanna
aachihma holissochittook.
Chikashshakaashoot
Savannah, Georgia aashacha
piini' anonka' binohmáakat
inchokka' falamattook aachi.

84

CHIIKI PÍLLA ÁYYA'SHAKAASH

Chikashsha mómaat hashi' fochik cho'ma kaniht kanallika ithánattook. Aba' pisahmat katihkma hilha, hokchi, ayoowa, owwata, cha nani' hotosi' ayaka ithanattook miya. Aba' Bínni'li'akoot naamóma chokmakat ímmayyattook.

85

Mr. Wesleyat imasilhhakat "Kanahmat aba' ántat naamóma apiisachik<u>a</u> hashith<u>á</u>nataa?" Tashka Chikashsha chaffa'at falamat aachikat "Nanna oshta' holitto'paat aba; hashi', hoshonti', shotik bosholli', micha Aba' Bínni'li' il<u>i</u>yimmi." aashttook.

Aba' Bínni'li'at hashi' cha naaholitto'pa' ikbi imasilhhahm<u>a</u> tashkaat kanookyaat Aba' Bínni'li' pisa'hi ki'yaam ittibaachaffattook. Aba' Bínni'li'at yaakni' ishthootobashttook<u>a</u> ittibaachaffattook miya.

Mr. Wesleyat tashk<u>a</u> imasilhhahmat Aba' Bínni'li'at tashk<u>a</u> atoonitok<u>a</u> tashkaat ittibikaash naki' lawaat pitwakohahookya iknalhlhokittookat ikhottopokittook<u>a</u> iman<u>o</u>ttook.

"Salla'chihookmat, salla'shkikat hattak finha' chohmi salla'ch<u>o</u>. Saokch<u>á</u>a bannahookm<u>a</u> saokch<u>á</u>a. Intanap lawa' akpisokitok<u>a</u> m<u>ó</u>ma aba'hi bíyyi'ka," tashkaat aashtok.

Imasilhhakat kat<u>i</u>shch<u>i</u> nannakaash hashithana'hi biyyi'kak<u>a</u> anompa falammichikat ponchokka' iilakat ilith<u>á</u>nattook. Hattak himitta' poyana hattak sipokni'at naaith<u>á</u>na ímmayya. Hoom<u>ó</u>mat ikitha'nohookya kanihmo'si'at himittakat <u>í</u>'mahm<u>a</u> Aba' Bínni'li'at p<u>a</u>fit apiisachicha imaabachi. Hooith<u>á</u>nana p<u>o</u>hattak sipokni'at yahmi akitha'nohootok<u>o</u>.

NOW THAT YOU KNOW THESE CHIKASHA STORIES, IT IS YOUR TURN. USE THESE PAGES TO DRAW AND WRITE YOUR STORY.